a ragged god

*poems & reflections
by dan turner*

apocryphile press
BERKELEY, CA

Apocryphile Press
1700 Shattuck Ave #81
Berkeley, CA 94709
www.apocryphile.org

© 2015 by Daniel Turner

All rights reserved. No part of this book may be reproduced, stored in a retrieval system, or transmitted in any form or by any means—electronic, mechanical, photocopy, recording, or otherwise—without written permission of the author and publisher, except for brief quotations in printed reviews.

Printed in the United States of America
ISBN 9781940671727

Back cover photo © 1993 by Dennis Ryan Kelly, Jr.

contents

— god —

If God 9
I'm Waiting 10
What Kind of God 11
Goddog 12
God Burdened 13
Are You There? 14
The Man 15
Windswept 17
A Past Thought 20

— family —

Three Generations 25
Meeting On a Day 26
Away from Home 28
Winter Memory Chicago 29
For Charlie 31
Alice, the Dog in Memoriam 32
My Two Sisters: For Terry and Nancy 33
This Body 34
The Children 36

— beauty —

White Bird 41
The Rebirth and Death of a Monastery 42
Sights on a Walk 43
The Prarie 46
Baja Reflection, 3-28-01 60

Thunder Ranges 62
The Sounds of Spring 63

— justice —

Memory and Past 69
Questions 70
One Night in Cambodia 71
Refugee Boy 73
Night in Nicaragua 74
El Pueblo de los Campos 75
The Women of Nicaragua 77
The Woman on the Judah St. Trolley, June 20, 2000 80

About the Author 82

DEDICATED

to the memory of my dear friend

STAN LUBARSKI

and with heartfelt thanks to my wife

ELIZABETH

god

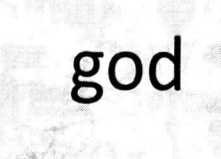

If God

If God's face was moist upon
    the morning
If he blinked away sleep
  and smiled when he saw me
I would love him.
    I would love him like the sun
    or a leaf or a flower.
Like a bird would I love him.
If he rubbed his eyes on waking
    Oh, I would love him
Like a brother, like a sister, like a mother
    He would be loved then.

I'm Waiting

If I stood still, He would bump into me.
    I would not have to search Him out.
If I stood in this place,
    He could not miss me.
He would fall into me, arms awkward, eyes startled.
    He would laugh like a belch of surprise.
If I stood right here, and stretched to embrace.
    He would stumble into my arms.
I would hold Him, my pilgrim God.
    And laugh at all His folly for my sake
And weep at all His pain
    for my sake.
If I but stood where I am now
    Wouldn't He stumble into me.
My God, my pilgrim wanderer?
    I'm waiting.

What Kind of God

I worship a ragged God, a dusty deity
    who staggered out of the desert
    dragging darkness after Him
I love a burdened God,
    She-heavy with all the world's births.
Embracing those born out of time, the castaways
    the bastards, the peculiar, the queer.
She is hounded through the streets
    by her hateful children whom she simply loves.
My God is not perfect,
    seeking darkness...to scatter Light.
    To scatter Light.

Godog

I always wanted to love You like a dog loves.
    The most accessible sweet being.
Is this why your name backwards means what it means?

God Burdened

I have carried the burden of God within me
    Weighing me down
Through the dark bottomless pool of struggles.

The weight of God has dragged at me,
    Suffocated me, denied me flight
When I sought higher destinies.

A sack of stones held me firm
    But a light beckoned.
I wondered then whose weight I bore.

Until I felt the heaviness was all my own,
    My own voice masquerading divinity
A created god of dubious intent.

Until I knew that God has no weight
    His burden light, Her harness joyful.
I soared then, untethered by my own limits.

Are You There

Were I born in the mountains
would I yearn to go higher,
would I go to the final reach, off the earth?
Were you there, my God, I would dare so.

Were I weaned in the desert
would I seek the pathless wastes,
would I lose myself to the sun,
sink into dust?
Were you there, my God, I would lose all of me.

Were the mountains in my soul and deserts in my heart,
would I course the trackless ways
to touch the high, holy image of your face?

If you were there...
Are you there?

The Man

I climbed an ancient weathered hill
   —windblown, bare and high,
When I saw the figure of a man outlined against the sky,
And the wind that whipped the hilltop's crest
   gave a mournful sigh.

This man was tall and strong, but still,
   most gentle to behold.
His face was strange and had the look of one
   both young and old.
And the wind that shook the odd-shaped tree
   felt so bitter cold.

He saw me as I stood and a smile crossed his face.
It wasn't broad but very slight
   and seemed to warm that place.
And the wind now touched the grass-blade tips
   with a soft, caressing grace.

I did not know this quiet man, yet I knew him all my life.
He was there beside me as I faced the world's strife.
And the wind was sharp across the hill
   like a newly whetted knife.

a ragged god

His look contained all wondrous things,
   but still seemed hurt and sad,
As though it held a burning love
   in golden vestments clad
That thoughtless men would brush aside,
   men both good and bad.

This gentle, loving face showed forth glory and great loss.
And then I knew just who He was.
   How had I been so gross?
From the "odd-shaped tree," behind the Man,
   fell the shadow of the Cross.

Windswept

All across the hill they were standing
   Hooded figures in silent conversation with God.
The watched the sun, splendid in its red-fire,
   Paint lingering cloud-tufts with careless strokes.
Swishes of pink, light blendings of orange
   Upon the sky's blue canvas.

They knew whose hand moved this brush
   To set the evening light in such grandeur.
Silently, as the sun sets silently, they walked
   With rustling steps, with guarded eyes,
   To sing the praises of God.

A day ended and evening came upon the men of prayer.
   But their souls remained in the twilight of eternity.

* * *

I walked in a high field under
   the crystal darkness of night.
   My view of the sky was vast and panoramic.

It seemed as though the black dome of the hallowed hour
   had been pierced a thousand times,

And that the stars were but the holes
  where the light of Heaven strained through
  in spangled clarity.

The moon was so bright as to give light by which
  one could read.
Standing there, a solitary figure in company with
  the pervading stillness,
My thoughts roamed free, climbed the ladders
  of celestial beauty
And drifted on the whisperings of invisible mist.

The wind caught up the ends of my scapular,
  seeking to fling them into the ebony emptiness.
But they merely drew a darker picture
  upon the ground,
Where their shadow kept the dusty brightness
  of the moon from gilding the earth
  with its silver-white magic.
And I was humbled by Him who had given
  this majesty to the sight of man
  for his fruitful contemplation.

* * *

I can hear the sad whispering moan
  of the wind

As it sweeps across the barren hill
   like a lost soul in search of peace.
Aimlessly wandering over the land,
   chanting its low mournful psalm.
The crying despair is rent from the
   darkest chambers of the heart.
The floodtide of anguish carries it recklessly
   onward
Until it catches on a branch of driftwood
   and floats safely to land, to peace, to
     solitude.
And the branch is the shape of the cross.

A Past Thought

From forgotten shores I heard
    the small voice call.
An echoing wave across
    the blackness of the past.
A throbbing cry, it grew in power
    till at last—
Its thunder shook the temple
    of my thought.

With eagerness and searching it traced
    the old familiar paths
To find them barren
    of everything it knew.
And in their place a strangeness
    strongly grew,
Thrusting walls of strength where weakness
    once had ruled.

An urgent cry it bellowed,
    and in fear
It sought an old wound—
    one that had not healed.
But to each beseeching sound
    I did not yield.

My life, my love, my soul
    had found new fields.
        —And then, with tears, I prayed.

family

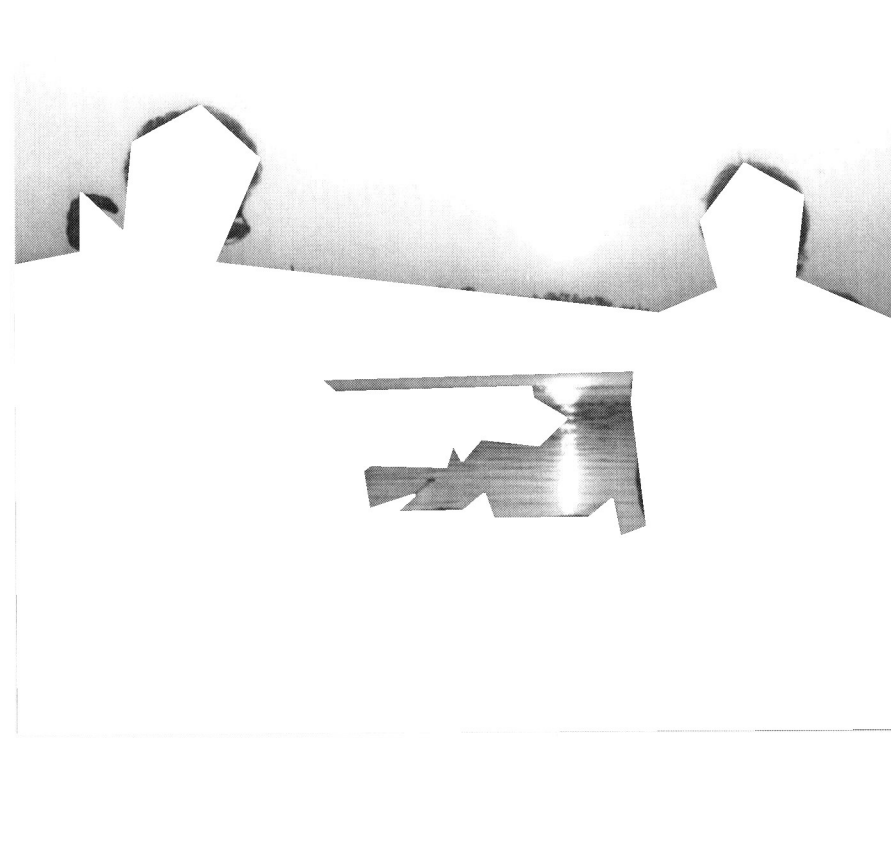

Three Generations

I send words to my brother, my sisters:
    we are all that's left, but not the leavings,
Of those who are now shadows and memory,
    once of substance so strong.

Once they were un-misted by remembrance.
    For they were sound and smell and feelings.
They—oh they—were our earth
    Our springing forth.

They—oh they—were sky for us to reach
    And carried us until our feet became ground,
Then the future ghost of memory rose up
    Until they—oh they—became
        our clouds of remembrance.

We are all that's left, but not the leavings.
    Memory ghosts creep up the legs of our children.

Meeting On a Day

Someday I would like to meet my Mom
    walking along the brown river in the town
    where she was born.
I can see her raven hair catching the sun
    like glass glittering through it
    or crystals woven among the tresses.

She is young and on the edge of womanhood
    so she walks loosely as a tomboy
her dress cotton, faded and hand-me-down.

She laughs out loud at a random thought
    of her family full of older sisters and brothers older
    except for the youngest whom she laughs over.

She warms to him her favorite
    and children play in her river-images
    but she is yet too young for them.

But many things she imagines then:
    a husband, how will he be
    and will their children be beautiful and smart?

Then in a moment she sees far ahead
—beyond her death,
    and I see back before my birth.
    We meet in that timeless space
        that never happened.
I walk down the river to her walking up.
    She tilts her head and squints her eye
    like she knows me but does not.

"I thought you would look this way,"
    I tell her and she smiles not moving.
    She senses the river and time in that moment.
A chill shivers her as I come from a time
    after her death, where her fantasies ended.
    She senses me as a strange thought and not real.

Then I am gone and she laughs again.
    I was never there, only a trick of river light.
    She wonders of things
      beyond the brown river flowing
    ...that wait for her somewhere.

Away from Home

These rain soaked streets carry no memory of my mother.
    They are dark but light circles there and beyond there.
And evening curves watchfully over all these shadow ways.

These streets carry no memory of my mother
    Nor have they felt the pressure of her feet.
Her voice has never echoed down these streets
    Nor her form seen moving against their length.

It is to other streets I must go
    to find her in my heart's eye.
To other streets she belongs,
    her children walking by her side.
To home streets is given the sound of her laughter
    and the sight of her embrace.

But I am not there to claim her memory
    which moves as a mist in the night.

Winter Memory Chicago

   Winter in mid-childhood.
I would walk home ending long hours
   of sledding and snowballing.
It was early dark. In the homes along
   the way, the lamps were already lit.
The light spilled out of their windows
   pooling orange on the snow, pooling yellow,
          pooling circles of gold.

   Squinting my eyes as I walked,
   I saw myself still and the houses
   slowly moving past me on my right.
   I thought if I stepped into
one of those haloes of light, I would be etherealized,
   inhaled by the night, becoming luminescent
   as the Moon, or swiped across
that splendent journey of stars—our high Milky Road.
   And in that black, brittle cold of night,
   I would know the secrets of the
          Earth-vigilant stars.

   But the passage of the houses would stop.
And as I had not entered the ponds of light
shimmering on the snow-lawns, I felt the dampness

and the chill urging me home. There I went to the
embrace of warmth, the smiles of my sisters,
   the humor of my brother, the reassurance of my Dad
   rattling the evening paper and
the steam from my Mom's cooking enwrapping us
with love moist and verdant—green,
where all else in the night outside was white
      to the edge of the dark, rippling, inland sea.

For Charlie

Charlie, you can hear the far cries
    of your ancestors now.
They are running across the endless fields
    and through the great trees of your homeland.

They are gathering.

Charles, their long cries will soon be
    yelps and barks of welcome.
Sniffs and licks and sweet bites of greeting.

Your ancestors are gathering.

Charlie, you will soon be home in the land
    of your dreamtime journeys
To await in joy the coming of your family
    Who now in sadness say goodbye.

Charlie, your ancestors are gathering. Listen.

Alice, the Dog In Memoriam

Alice and Charlie   now
are bumping noses   now
circling each other   now
dog yipping to the sky   now
deliriously happy   now

Separation, darkness
Are no more   now

My Two Sisters: For Terry and Nancy

I thought to bring them jewels
    But none would match their worth,
For kindness done, for unflinching support,
    for hearts opened:
There are no jewels to give
    for love.

I wished to bring them gold or silvered objects
    But what are these?
Among laughter shared and books and movies
    And long memories:
There are no precious metals
    for the sharing of lives.

So I gave them words that are free,
    Costing nothing, poor currency:
Given deep generosity and caring
    and sistering of one:
There are no words.
    for two priceless Spirits, always.

This Body

When it was young, this body crouched
    long at the curb
As clear water rippled toward
    the sewer's mouth.
As clear water yet unsullied
    sparkled with captured sunlight
Like golden spiders dancing
    ...like spiders of gold leaping.

This body drank the rain stream from the night
    carrying the day's glitter on its limpid skin.
This body when it was young became
    a light dancing...a light leaping.

When it was young...
    when it was young
This body became all.

The Children

There were two children walking up the old farm road
   that bleached white in the hot brightness
   of the Autumn sun.
One was older, a few years, and taller—a boy,
   and the other was small and pretty—a girl.
And they were wise in the wisdom that is youth's,
   for their knowledge was the simple understanding
     of children
   to see through the prejudice
     and sophistication of the years.
They were not yet trained to hate, to scorn, to mock.
Their naiveté was deep and held within its bounds
   the holiness of the Humble Man.

Home to lunch from the one-room school house
   standing strangely silent for a fleeting hour.
The heat of noon gave an odd metallic sound
   to the cry of the crow and the drone of the fly.
The children dallied as they walked along the road.
The boy flicked twigs across the way to send up
   little spurts of dust in clever billows.
The little girl laughed encouragingly.
Trees that bordered their path were many-hued
   by the work of diligent Fall.

And the small girl delighted in picking leaves
  with bright colors,
And in holding them to her heart
  as if to fully partake of their beauty.
Or, perhaps, to think sadly of the cold winter days
  which would rob the trees of their glorious raiment.
But then, pressed between the pages of a favorite book,
  she could take out this beauty
And relive in the fertile valley of her memory
  these days of God's gentle artistry.—
        She was a dreamer

The boy, seeing her expression drift into other climes,
  broke in upon these thoughts,
With eager acrobatics from the trees, with funny faces.
  The girl laughed, for she sought to please,
And her laughter was water rippling over pebbled pearls.
But deftly a bold gust of wind snatched the beauty
  she held in her hands
And flung it with fluttering disdain far from her
  child grasp.
She winced, for, even in her tender years, she felt
  the pain that comes from wanton waste.—
        She was a dreamer.

beauty

White Bird

White bird flashing bright
    above the green meadow
Carrying the morning sun
    upon its back—in a whirling of soundless ecstasy.

The Rebirth and Death of a Monastery

The corridors were dark sometimes and they held
    the forest silence in their arms.
Then came life in white, straight steps to try
    the quiet of the halls.
In swift white forms, clusters were carried
    through the dark embrace.
Like single souls cupped in a mother's arms,
    the fragile shadows were warmed with ancient stone.
Men and souls passed by, and on, and on,
   with muffled steps,
    which told of places to go and destinies to reach.

II

The corridors are dark again and hold a deeper silence
    in their embrace.
The steps that carried souls with straight, white grace
    have found the destinies and have reached the place.
The halls have other feet to try the stillness now
    and other shadows to feel the hallowed arms.
Life, that once with quickened step,
   did know the darkness
   and the silence of the halls,
Has now been replaced by death,
   and only evening echoes in
    the place and only spirits know the ancient walls.

Sights on a Walk

Often, when the solitude of my person grows
    upon me,
I find myself walking up one of the weathered roads
    that twists silently away from the monastery.
The mind of my heart is filled with varied
    thoughts.
And I come into a place peopled with the blue and
    white and gold of young creation.
As I walk through these late summer
    buddings,
They softly chastise my feet with gentle reprimand
    for invading their verdant privacy.
And this field, in which I walk, rises before me
    to the limits of horizon—
As though there were nothing beyond but the loneliness
    of space, of everlasting emptiness.
Yet, from the very top, where the sky joins the earth,
I see a brilliant whiteness barely peaking.
It is the combed silkiness of new cotton,
Or it is the hoary heads of the venerable patriarchs
    slowly rising from sleep
To see if their children of the valleys and
    hills

a ragged god

Are to the age-old work of praise and struggle
    which they began so many eons ago.
Quickly I run to where the gradual rise achieves
    its peak.
And I stop breathless with the sight that falls
    before me in undulating waves of land.
For the fields climb and drop down into the
    valley of the Great River.
There, protected by the mighty bluffs which rise
    boldly around it, is a small town quietly
    resting in an almost faery setting.
And here it is I see from where the whiteness
    came.
A shining silver sea of mist as thick as the
    clouds of heaven,
Hovers matronly over its legend town, making
    everything that stands behind it nonexistent.
But the small town can be seen in a veiled gray—
As though the mist favored it for the eyes of the
traveler to look upon.
Then from the East, the Sun, hidden behind dappled
    clouds,
Diffuses its brilliance over the valleys so that only
    bright fingers of light reach down to touch
    the land awake,

And flicker in the leaves of the weary, ancient trees.
And my solitude has departed, for His creation has
    filled my heart.
Now the pictures fade. The covers of my heart close
    on this chapter for another year.
New things will be added and new faces will appear.
      but let me not forget the old ones I hold so dear.

And the snow drifts again,
   covering the footprints of remembrance.

The Prairie

I looked out through the wooden fence and saw the prairie beyond, lucent and green. Insect noise quivered in the dwarfed jungle of weeds and grass. Sound shook the wildflowers rather than wind, the insect song being the more noticeable. Numberless creatures clung to the wiggling stalks trying to pollinate or devour. The prairie shimmered in waves harmonizing sound, light and movement. It preened itself; it breathed.

The sign of an intruder to the prairie was immediately evident like an invisible hand drawing itself discordantly across the rhythmic waves. It signaled a cat or a small dog that couldn't top the prairie growth. A shout from me and they stopped for long seconds, then resumed. A rock thrown near them caused an erratic change of direction. Sometimes I would lie in line with their course through the prairie, and if I was downwind they would continue unsuspecting until a parting of the low jungle growth in their track revealed my grinning head like a terrible stone god waiting to destroy. The cats would go straight up in the air and disappear before landing. The dogs would go stiff-legged and bark, startled and angry, like it wasn't fair of me to have scared them. If the dog knew me, he would whine and lick my face. If not, his ears would go back, tail cover his butt and he'd scoot away slightly sideways.

My eyes were at ground level for long stretches of time in the summer afternoons in my childhood. I can still recall the hot sun on my back as I lay belly-down in the prairie, getting an ant's eye view of the world. I saw how grass on its level was as strong and supple as trees were on theirs. I got a sense of perspective by thrusting my head everywhere I could and microscoping my eyes to the small world beneath my nose. Passing neighbors were accustomed to seeing me lying still and face down among the weeds and grasses of the prairie. They wanted the reassurance of movement to dispel their quick fear of death that my quiet form evoked. When I sensed them staring, I would pull up my head and smile to send them on their way, wondering about me.

My buddies and I liked to dig in the prairie. The feel of my small entrenching tool as it cut through the sandy loam was very satisfying. In the winter, I could hardly wait until spring and summer when I would be able to invade the prairie with my pals and start the digging again. Its surface was the forgiving hide of an old and earthy friend who was patiently guiding me through my childhood. My relationship to this plot of ground was, at times, womb-like. I was constantly burying myself in it. I dug holes and trenches, roofed them over with wood and sod and then would lie silent in the moist darkness.

Day after day in the prairie never bored me. It was alive and there were possibilities undreamed of out there. We were simpatico, the prairie and I: it gave and I took; it provided and I used. Occasionally, this would reverse. But mostly I was the receiver of prairie gifts, and that's as it should be. I was younger, far less experienced, needing encounters, and the prairie somehow sensed this. It enfolded me into its secrets, making revelations that stayed with me the rest of my life.

The prairie had a rich personality of soils. There was black, gold, red and gray. It would produce water, if you dug deeply enough, and other mysterious things. I remember one time when I was around ten digging quietly by myself. No great project in mind. I was probably just going to dig a narrow trench and throw dirt over myself for the grand feel of it. I had cut through two or three feet of prairie soil when I noticed a seam of white separating the sand level from the clay dirt. I inspected closely with my fingers and discovered chalky fossils, small seashells and other twisted and fluted creatures from a past before me or my ancestors. I was awed. With reverence, I tried to extract some of these remains, but they easily crumbled in my hands. I had been told that where we lived was once at the bottom of Lake Michigan in prehistoric times. It was bedded now two miles to the east.

I told a couple of my friends of my discovery, but they weren't too interested. But I was—these were fossils! Even at ten, I knew about things like this because I read a lot. This discovery made the prairie more ancient and therefore more sacred than I had imagined. It had changed itself over the millennia but held the secret of its former existence in its earthly folds. That was exciting, and my discovery bonded me more closely to this old patch of earth. I shoveled the soil back over the trench. But that spot always remained a place of reverence for me. And in the spring, I would transplant wild daisies and clover over the place of the fossils.

So, I lived my childhood among the folds of prairie earth thick with weeds and grass, with occasional wildflowers exploding like small epiphanies of color in the predominant green. Bright, bright greenness, it shimmered in the stalks and stems of everything that grew there. It was more than color. Green was an entity. It had substance. And deeply, beyond all appearances, it had language. In that prairie was the possibility of an understanding that reached so far behind history, beyond the awareness of reason, that it connected back to a time when our infant species was held in the lap of the great Mother—with all the other species. And together we knew wind and movement and shadow and light as language. This is what the Prairie taught me.

One night in a summer, when I was nine or ten, the moon was so bright that wherever a shaft of its light fell, it burned away the darkness and everything around it glowed. It was hot indoors. There was no air-conditioning then. I was restless through the night until a calmness overtook me. I felt a deep quiet surrounding me. I got out of bed, walked through the kitchen and out the back door onto the porch. Even the floorboards felt warm to my feet. But as I walked down the steps into our backyard, a flutter of a breeze brought some relief from the heat.

I stood leaning on the fence looking out in the prairie blackness, scattered with pools of moon-bright. The calm and quiet maintained even in the light breeze. I waited. And then it came clear and only once: my name, "Dan!" was spoken out of the prairie's stillness. With that, I slipped from my standing form and slid across the tops of the tall grass and weeds. I dipped and twirled through the narrow plant paths, enraptured with the ease of my movement, not surprised at what was happening and still conscious of my body leaning on the fence looking out over the prairie. The same awareness that was moving me across the top of the prairie was there at the fence also. And when the breeze stopped, I slipped back into my form, turned from the fence and walked back into the house to my bed, smiling and with a new love beating inside my chest.

Ants overpopulated the sandy pathway through the prairie. They were endlessly fascinating, timeless workers, an inspiration to a lone boy on a hot afternoon in summer. I tried to will myself small in order to become the familiar of ants that nervously practiced their arts before my unblinking eyes. I scrutinized their characteristics, hoping that one ant would emerge as an individual with a special walk or an unusual antenna that I could remember and come to know as a friend. I used to whisper my name through the grass so the ants would get familiar with me and not fear my head when it came like a hairy meteor into their sandy world. The breath that pushed forth my name sent the ants and other nameless creatures tumbling and scurrying for their sand retreats. Sad to say, I never did get to know any ant as an individual pal, but then I never saw them all.

After watching them for long interludes, I was moved by their industry to pick up my entrenching tool and dig. Sometimes I'd dig a trench or just a hole deep enough to hang my head in to listen to the dull roar that emanated from it. I thought it came from deep in the earth, that things were moving and boiling down there like hot lava. The roaring was the signals sent up through hundreds of miles of earth. I felt connected to the whole globe in this way. Because the hole enabled me to hear the visceral rumbling of the entire planet, there developed a metaphysical bond between the earth and me, which made even stronger the physical bond I already had from walking, lying, rolling and burying myself in its folds of dirt and sand. This small stretch of prairie was my opening to the whole world: the mysterious forces beneath its crust and the jittering, flashing life above it.

I was amazed at the intricate symmetry of each weed head and flower I studied. I wondered how they could grow themselves into such perfect patterns of color and design. There was an inkling of some other powers at work here in the prairie. And sometimes I would get scared at these intimations and would have to stand up out of the weeds quickly. I felt like something was getting very close to me. Because I didn't know what it was, I experienced fright along with fascination. But there were other times when I would stay deep in the prairie grasses, ignoring the fright and hanging on. It was then that secrets opened to me that I did not understand at the time. Only later, as years went by, when there would be a green flash of memory, did I comprehend that being was resonating unto being. The basic relationship of sameness shared among all of us:

earth, weeds, bugs and me. I placed no hierarchy there because to do so would destroy the possibility of communication. I would not be able to see with the bug's eye nor hear the ancient talk of the earth nor feel the power the prairie held were I to establish various levels of being among all of us friends inhabiting that plot of ground.

At the end of summer, the prairie had worked itself dry. The stalks of the weeds were brittle and hurt if you stepped on them with your bare feet. The grass had lost its resilience and rested limply and brown on the prairie floor. Long before this, the wildflowers had released their bloom to the bright summer sun.

I matched the prairie with my mood of slow listlessness. The heat of August made us both quiet and pensive. School would be starting soon. There was nothing to do. I had scoured every inch of prairie earth from early spring to late summer. My verdant friend and I had exhausted ourselves in discovery and play. I waited for the doom to start after Labor Day.

Then, one night, a terrible thing happened. I awoke, hearing shouts and loud crackling. I figured someone was crushing orange crates, but it didn't make sense in the middle of the night. And then I smelled smoke and knew the prairie was on fire! I ran out the back porch and leaped to the yard just in time to see my Dad vault over the fence into the prairie like he'd been doing it all his life. And there was the prairie with flame moving from one end to the other. The wind was pushing the fire rapidly across the prairie floor. I started to get the backyard hose but realized it was too late. Where it had already burned, there were red and orange cinders like fairy fires hidden deep in the grass. But there were hundreds of them!

I was stunned and fascinated by the spectacle, and scared. What would happen to the prairie after the flames had consumed it? It would be dead! All the myriad insects curled crisply in death. What would there be left?

I saw Dad running around the far edge of the prairie where it had already burned—what was he doing? He was heading for the back yard of the building that bordered the prairie opposite of us. I saw another man just entering the gate in a hurry, as if trying to escape my Dad—and he was! I couldn't hear what was said because Dad was speaking in angry but quiet tones, while Mr. Harris' voice was excited and screeching. What happened was that he had set the fire. He was a mean old fart who didn't like us kids. He would complain about the noise we made and called the cops on us about once a month. He finally decided to ruin our fun by setting fire to our prairie. A neighbor told us later that Dad nailed Harris for his sneakiness and cowardice and warned him never to do anything like that again or he would answer to Dad for it. Mr. Harris squealed back that Dad had better not enter his yard or he would call the cops. Dad entered his yard. Mr. Harris did nothing: Dad had thoroughly scared him. He never bothered us or our prairie again. Dad was a hero to all the guys who played in the prairie. I glistened with pride whenever they would talk about him.

The next day I walked out into a seared and blackened space. It was still warm. Ash clouds spurted up wherever I stepped. It was awful. I cried because I thought I'd never see that vibrant, living friend again but only a barren patch of earth. My Mom and Dad tried to reassure me that the prairie would come back next spring, rich and green. But I didn't see how it could. It had been burnt to death.

The thing about the prairie in the spring (at least, before the fire) was that it seemed to bloom all at once, overnight—not gradually. One Saturday in spring, I would look over the slat fence and there it would be: waving, beckoning, all the green glorious life of a new prairie! It would sneak up on me like that every spring, growing furiously while I was still in school; pushing up taller and taller while I slept. Until that splendid Saturday morning in spring when it unfolded all at once: "Here I am. Come and get me!"

Once I was so excited at the sight of its luxuriance that I reared back, ran for the fence and dove head first, clearing it by a foot. I belly-flopped into the prairie, cushioned by the grass, the plants and soft ground. I swam in its welcome!

But that fall, after the fire, was sad for me because every day there was the blackened reminder of an adult's violation of our kids' paradise. Winter wasn't much better. My buddies and I were able to build our snow forts and snowmen, but they were gray and so were we.

Eventually the warm winds started blowing in after Easter. The snow melted in rills and rivulets all over the prairie, like it did every spring. The ground was still black but less so. The music of water running down slopes, curving around rocks and splashing against everything in its path filled the air above the prairie like always. I would hunker down on a Saturday morning in early April, watching the sunlight sparkle off the rushets of water like clouds of daylight fireflies, like diamonds, like springtime ice!

There was such a freshness that filled my being as I inhaled all that prairie cleansed by fire and now by water. Green began to appear here and there among the summer's ashes and the smell of coming spring swept away all dour thoughts. Perhaps the prairie would return as before.

In previous springtimes, I would crawl alongside the narrow streamlets to see where they went. Some snaked through the grasses to form pools a foot or so wide and several inches deep. A few of these would survive until summer, shaded by the tall plants or one of the two cottonwood trees that bordered the prairie. I would unexpectedly discover one of these pools by the shock of stepping into it. It was a thrill to see that it was still there from early spring. Peering into it, I saw lots of specks skittering about eager to join their larger insect kin among the wilds of the prairie.

Other small streams disappeared into holes in the ground almost as if the lips of the earth opened to drink in the draughts of spring. I would dig into these loamy mouths to see how far I could follow the disappearing water, but the earth kept crumbling over the narrow tubes so I would stop. I didn't want to pursue too far because I sensed this an unwelcome intrusion into a secret. I liked to imagine that all these waters drained into a dark, cavernous belly beneath the prairie, to be distilled into an elixir that could sate only the plants, weeds and flowers that grew here. A water unique to this piece of earth alone.

There was one time, however, when the hole into which

the water disappeared did not crumble over. Instead, after a foot of digging, it opened out and my hand plunged downward into a cold pool. As I pulled away the covering earth, there it was: a clear crystal pool of liquid, lined with fine sand and small white stones. I had broken into a hidden place that I should not know about. This tiny pool was so beautiful I wondered how long it had been there—a mere foot below the ground. I carefully removed the pieces of sod that had fallen in. I searched for branches and stones for support and laid sod over the pool until it looked natural again. This was near the eastern edge of the prairie. We kids didn't play there much because it was too near the sidewalk. Whenever I was in the prairie after that, the side of my body that faced the direction of the hidden pool sensed it. There would be a twinge or stitch on that side of me, and I knew that was a reminder to keep secret another gift from the prairie. And I did, until now.

Adults seldom entered our prairie. It was weed-infested. The ground dipped and rose irregularly, making it hard to negotiate, unless, like we denizens, one knew it well. Adults did not catch the magic of the prairie and usually stayed out of it. Occasionally, one would venture into it. One day, Mrs. Eady did so—a large woman in her 40s who wore loose cotton dresses to cover her expansive frame. They flapped like flags upon her whenever she walked in a hurry, which she was doing the day she took the lone path that cut through the prairie.

The week previous, my friends and I had been burrowing into the earth with mighty effort. We had constructed an intricate series of trenches covering a good quarter of the prairie. We roofed them over with old planks from our building's back porch, which was being rebuilt. Over the planks we laid the thick sod that had previously covered the ground. The unpracticed eye could not detect that the green, grassy prairie was undermined by subterranean passageways. This made it all the more exciting to us. We felt ourselves as native to this piece of earth: we lived in it, not just on it.

Once in a while, we'd pick tomatoes from one of the victory gardens nearby (planted during WWII) and hurl them at passing cars, including cop cars. The sound and splatter were viscerally satisfying. As the cars stopped upon impact and the drivers emerged to wring our necks, we would tear off into the prairie and wriggle down one of our hidden holes into the tunnels below, like the little rats we were. We could hear the drivers walking above us, trickles of dirt landing on our heads where they walked or stood. They were baffled: they saw us run to the prairie and then disappear in the tall growth and we did not emerge anywhere! I heard one perplexed motorist stating: "It's like they disappeared into the air!" He just had his direction wrong.

Anyway, back to Mrs. Eady crossing our prairie like a three-masted man-o'-war sailing down the path. When I saw her, she was about to cross our tunnels which we had constructed under the path, because it would be neat to be down there with people walking above us thinking they were on solid ground. People could walk across but not Mrs. Eady! We had not counted on supporting her tonnage. I watched but could not speak, waiting for the crack of doom. But she sailed right by, flags flapping proudly. She made it! The roofs held! We were engineers!

I went back to counting ants or whatever I was doing. Mrs. Eady returned, probably from the store. I paid no attention until lightning struck. I heard a sharp crack and then another, followed by a roar as Mrs. Eady slowly sunk into the ground amidst splintering wood and billows of dust, her flags hanging limply. I couldn't move. Through the clouds of destruction, she riveted me with her eyes, and I could have sworn they were red. "You damned little runts," she bellowed. Of course, compared to her most people were runts. I got the message, however, and ran rabbit-fast for Mom, who had heard the noise. She met me on the porch; I could only point. Mom ran out with me behind. We helped Mrs. Eady unplug herself from the main hall of our underground quarters.

Mrs. Eady demanded that we kids should be arrested, even though I was the only one there. She called for the destruction of the tunnels. Mom kept trying to soothe her and pointed out that the prairie was where all the kids played and they didn't mean for this to happen. She steered the soiled, swearing, once proud galleon home.

Mom told me that we kids had to fill in the tunnels. In the light of what happened, we had to agree. The next day, the catacombs disappeared as we pulled up sod and planks. It was fun though—we were playing with our prairie friend and just re-altering her forgiving surface again. But not quite completely. The idea of a communal hole in the ground was too great to let go. So, under cover of weeds, we laid a double thickness of planks over a deep hole that would accommodate five sitting boys. This was done in a remote corner of the prairie. Five of us put all of our weight on the roof. We got two of the biggest guys in our group to stand on it while three of us climbed on top of them, trying to duplicate the weight of the unhappy Mrs. Eady. One of us down below shouted up the effects of our overhead trompings—there were none. That hole remained for years. Most of us forgot about it over time. But it never caved in. Once when I was an adult living in another city, I woke up with a start, remembering the hole and fearful that some unsuspecting person might fall through. But by then, as I quickly recalled, the prairie was no more. A house had been built upon it. Overnight she disappeared. All of that familiarity was gouged away, and a hole deeper and larger than any we kids had dug yawned at our backyard fence. Never again would I creep out at night and glide mystically through its cluttered population of grass, weeds and flowers. I would not sit in a mesmerized state listening to its sounds, staring at its microcosmic diversity.

But I grew up and out of that Prairie and pursued different places in other parts of the city and, eventually, in other parts of the world. They were fascinating. They offered the exotic. They provided the enticements of adventure. But not one of them held me to this earth with the endearing embrace of my Prairie—now long buried under the builder's bricks and mortar. None of those exciting places of my later years' wandering taught me more about my oneness with nature, my kinship with all beings, my place in the universe than the Prairie....She was my Buddha!

Baja Reflection, 3-28-01

The Baja makes one accustomed to beauty: awesome cliffs, striking rock formations, arches hollowed through massive walls of stone, a sea whose contrasts of all the ranges of blue and green become the expected—but never the commonplace. There is nothing common about the Baja and its sea. But I wanted some distance from it in order to reflect more independently upon what I saw and felt without the pulsing insistence of its beauty. I wanted to embrace only a segment in my writing and see in it the expression of the whole. In this way, the Baja, which is too much for anyone, can be accepted in human-sized portions and held as a small jewel to be turned in the hand without its beauty being diminished, only made more attainable.

And so, I could express the flight of one bird or a squadron of pelicans skimming low across the water, each in sync with each. Or the smell of the desert as burnt salt, in a heat-blasted landscape where everything looks dry and dead, yet everything lives. Or its resemblance to an old man's junkyard scattered with blackened machine parts. Or tell of the solitary feeling that comes when, as far as you can see, there is brush and cactus and forbidding mountains and hidden water. In the past, such places bred prophets and mystics: men driven beyond the accepted norms by the desert sun and the scarcity of everything except the burning beauty of a life centered on Mystery.

But I will write about a single bird on Carmen Island. He was a blue heron, skinny by any definition but beautiful to any eyes attached to a soul. He inhabited a small, marshy area about 100 yards behind our tent. This was surprising in such desert surroundings. A small dark pond of brackish water was his only source of drinking and meditation. Each morning, he would stretch his long neck and equally long beak to break his abstinence of water with a sip. And then in a stillness of rocks, he would stand contemplating the little pond and the deeper significance it held for him. I wondered about his pond: how could it sustain him with water; what kept it from drying up? It must have been dew dripping from the surrounding plants in the morning.

I would watch him from a respectful distance. Each time I was moved by a sense of prayer that his spare silhouette conveyed to me, and I loved him.

After his quiet and careful pondering, he would lift off from the edge of his hermitage. So easefully did he move that his legs reached up and up, and his feet did not seem to leave the rock he stood upon until he was high in flight. His great wings would stretch to welcome the day, and with a gesture of embrace, would carry him silently across the desert island to the Sea of Cortez. From its depth the great darkness of leviathan was slowly rising to that level where water becomes air. Like a promontory newly born, its curved back broke the surface and erupted in spume with a sigh releasing secrets from the deeps.

The heron-shadow crossed over the whale and the sea; crossed over the desert to the west and in a graceful arc flew into the circle of the sun, giving honor to all by its solitary existence.

Thunder Ranges

It was night upon the monastic hill.
    The stars poked into the darkness
    were the finger holes of heaven.
In clearness was all the sky
    with the brightness of ebony,
    flecked with vagrant sparks.
The West held to the horizon giants,
    Mountains of mist that rose in a great range
    stretching to north and south.
Clouds volcanic against the lucent night,
    dark monolithic monsters
    with hewn heads of ancient thought.
Lightning in pulsating splashes struck up
    from the bowels of night
    and stunned the primal faces with light.
Again, then again. All in silence and in power
    worked the fulminations
    their recurrent sacrifice to obscurity.

The Sounds of Spring

He stood on the road before me,
    A small and frail thing,
And with childlike wisdom he asked me
    "What are the sounds of spring?"

He did not ask what changes;
    What will come or what will go.
But simply, "What are the sounds?"
    For this is all he wished to know.

Oh, child close beside me,
    You're the offspring of my soul.
You're my passing youth that leaves me
    In the steady, yearly toll.

And, so you ask for the sounds:
    Well, now, listen and you will hear
The songs, the sounds, and the music
    Of this growing time of year.

Do you hear that harsh and cracking sound?
    There's one you ought to know.
It's the cry of that glistening blackbird,
    The shrill music of the crow.

a ragged god

You can see him sharp against the blue
   As he glides in the heat of the day.
His shrill and shattering echoes
   Frighten winter away.

The gushing of an early stream
   The foaming waters' ride.
The lowing of a spotted cow
   On a sloping hillside.

The winds on the plains; the winds in the trees;
   Wind of a thousand words.
The music of water; rippling of grass;
   The wild songs of the birds.

The thick dark earth as it opens up
   To the thrust of growing things.
A tractor, turning furrows...
   These are the sounds of spring.

Day upon day their music grows
   As winter slides to the sea.
These are the sounds that lift man up
   And let his soul roam free.

Listen to them closely, lad,
    They are a symphony for a king,
But we in our human ignorance
    Simply call them the "Sounds of Spring."

justice

Memory and Past

Do we look for the past in towns dwindling to dust
   from too much history and too little future?
Do we look for the past within ourselves,
   seeking memories that stir the blood
     and trouble the emotions?
Either way, but living memory outlives
   the buildings, backyards
     and lonely streets of youth.
Living memory voices the questions for the past,
   while the answers lie always in the heart.
Forgetfulness is locked in the wooden embrace of houses
   once thought everlasting on streets
     stretching to horizons.
Forgetfulness was never housed in a heart that cared.
   Only remembrance overburdened that lonely space.
A dearth of memory is not possessed by one who suffers.
   Forgetfulness would be a blessing.
It is remembering we seek to escape.

Questions

From where comes the anger that I harbor
    in my breast like fire?

Was it born a spark in some forgotten past,
    nurtured carefully?

Is it old? Is it fed
    the fuel of each day's woes?

Or is it a slumbering conflagration
    waiting for the breach to flare forth into flame?

If it is unleashed will it go about
    devouring, destroying?

This anger: Is it a bowl
    of the world's hurts—not just mine?

Must it burn in me
    that I not forget the forgotten?

Is it justice crying in my heart:
    Remember, Remember?

And then what...when I have remembered?

One Night in Cambodia

One night in Cambodia
    I slept in a broken temple
    in a moon-silvered jungle under a
black sky. The sounds of dragons slithering and tigers creeping through a dreamland.

One hot night in Cambodia
    I awoke in the jungle knowing that
    every dream has a place
where it exists.

In Cambodia one night
    I knew that death was out there in the jungle fringe but not for me. It could have been. But not for me.

In the jungle one night in Cambodia
    under a burning moon I heard God moan.

In a night black with heat in Cambodia
    I heard the cries of the people like whispered prayers slithering and creeping through the jungle darkness.

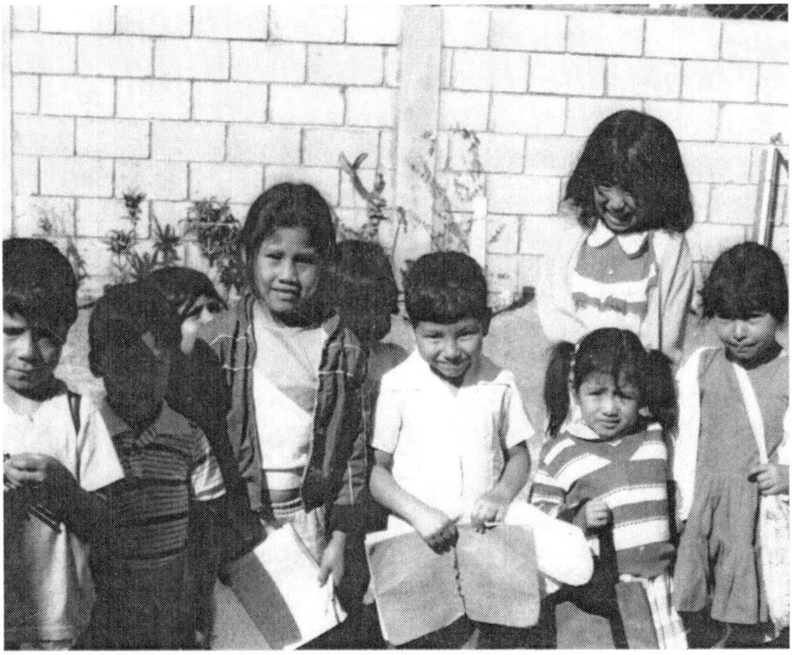

Refugee Boy

He came from his mother into a child-choked land
    But he was never born.

He moved as a shadow along the edges
   among brothers, sisters,
      countless cousins.

He was tribe. He was family.
   Only a small head shining among so
      many. He knew not who he was.

One day he stood near a tree alone.
   One day he touched the tree.
      One day he leaned against it

And said: "I am that which stands before this tree!"
   Startled, he tucked that knowing deep into his heart...
      and trembled.

Night in Nicaragua

For so long he had heard music coming unbidden,
    wisps of tunes out of the smoke.
A soundless music that welled up from his heart
    he would stop arrested in his movement.
Tracing the errant strands to a source
    deep within himself.
For so long he heard the music
    until one soundless night in Nicaragua
It ended...and wisdom began.

El Pueblo de los Campos

In a hidden place in my soul,
> there is a rainforest, there are mountains,
>> and beautiful villages
>> there are death and destruction and torture
>> and there are the people of the land,
>>> the campesinos.

In that place in my soul,
> there is El Salvador, Guatemala,
>> Nicaragua, and Honduras
> they are all there and
> they have defined me.

Sometimes in a night, in a day, alone,
> I see the faces of the women
>> in a quiet blue morning
> of smoky fires and tortillas and children
>> and the men
> walking thinly to the fields with machetes.

I hear their quiet words
> I see the deeps of sorrow in their eyes
>> the hard line of courage ridging their shoulders
>> and I long, long, long for them and their suffering.

At that place in my soul,
> I kneel before them in my sadness

and whisper: "Es usted Christus?"
    are you the Christ?
I worship the incarnate God they walk with
    into their blessed fields
    into the mountains and war
    and, too often, into death.
What can I do for them now?
send me a word that I may know
    or have they forgotten as I have
Send it and I will follow.

The Women of Nicaragua

The long road paved a straight line to the distant mountain in northern Nicaragua. The bus I was on hummed in the heat of noon. I nodded in and out of sleep, watching the road with lazy eyes until something up ahead arrested my gaze. It was like a rock at first, which began to take on a red hue as we approached it. I saw soon enough that it was a human figure sitting on the road. A woman wrapped in red cloth staring out across the fields. Her knees were pulled close to her chin. She was indeterminately old. Her hair was black with a silver sheen of age. She squatted there on the road with her gaze fixed to some space beyond the fields that extended to the horizon. I could not take my eyes from her. She was a peasant woman with strong, dark features. I had the sense of something elemental, even symbolic, about her as she sat silent and fixed and staring.

The bus swerved around her stoic figure. She did not move. There was a shift in my being. I felt deeply connected with this woman in red cloth. I did not know why at the time. By the end of my journey I understood better.

The women of Nicaragua articulate the anguished soul of their people: passionate with the sense of struggle, profound in their suffering. I saw these women in the towns creating normalcy in a society scourged by shortages and dancing ever closer to the brink of crushing poverty. I saw them on the roads without the aid of beast or cart carrying heavy burdens. And in the mountains where the battles waged, where the Contras struck as if like lightning from a clear sky, I saw the women of Nicaragua in deep sorrow.

They became the woman clothed in red on the roadway. Her name is Suffering, Campesino, Nicaragua!

In the village of Jinotega in the northern mountains of Nicaragua I sat in a small room stunned by these women as they told their stories to the group I traveled with. There were about twenty women who met daily to pray and to support one another. They called themselves: "The Mothers of the Heroes and Martyrs" because that is how they see their dead sons, daughters and husbands whom the Contras have killed. They told us in simple words how they lost those they loved: "They took my daughter from her school. I found her in the evening outside the village, raped and dead." "They beat my husband to death in the town square. He was a teacher." "The Contras raided our farm and took my old father. I have not seen him since."

It was suffering so deep that I could only listen without response. They prayed with us. We sang together holding hands. We ended with tears as we exchanged embraces in the kiss of peace.

I cannot convey what took place there in that small room. I am unable to express the pain of a spiritual beauty only achieved by tearing from the heart of one's soul that which one holds most dearly. A bloody void of incalculable darkness is left. The campesino woman cries in the hollow of that void for a God her church has not taught her about. The beauty comes when she does not destroy herself in hate or personal destruction. In the endless night that fills her soul, in the absence of all possibility of comfort, she knows that death is the only answer that will echo back her own cries. And she believes! Of course, there is a

God! Otherwise the world would be mad to expect her to survive such desolation. Only an unknowable God could expect such clay to sculpt itself into an image that one is tempted to worship for living such a faith as this. The campesino woman loves beyond the limits of the possible.

I can only write these words. The experience they express has not been mine but I know that people live it. Not how, but simply that they do. I saw them in Nicaragua, in El Salvador, in Guatemala and in Honduras. These strong, deep-eyed women with mahogany faces who embraced us. They told us to bring back the message of peace. They love the people of North America, they said. They fear our government for the killing it supports in their countries.

Woman in red cloth, gazing with the vision of eternity, you have changed me with your suffering. I know you now. You are "Campesino." You are "el Pueblo." You are the people and my own destiny.

The Woman on the Judah St. Trolley
San Francisco, June 20, 2000

She got on the N-Line trolley as it headed west along Judah St. She dropped into the seat, a burden of weariness that settled slowly. All of the lines on her face curved downward from the outer edges of her eyes to her mouth that had not entertained a smile in a spread of time. The bow of her lips sagged into sadness. She did not focus on anything. Her eyes stared into a gray distance without boundaries. She might have been attractive once, but even the hints of that struggled to survive in the present and lost. Slow, slow weariness is what she carried now. Her face framed her life, and it was one of failure and defeat—first theirs (whoever 'they' might be) and then hers. Hers being the final capitulation to what they did to her and what they didn't do for her by their complete indifference to her as a being that mattered.

I would like to have spoken kindly to her, but my own awkwardness prevented me and the possibility of embarrassment—hers and mine. I could only breathe a prayer to the Blessed Mother of us all to embrace her.

She got up after several stops and moved slowly, not with difficulty but with heaviness accumulated by the stunning fact that at last she was alone in the world. And all the life that swirled around her had nothing, nothing at all, to do with her.

As she stood at the trolley stop waiting to cross to the far side of the street, the trolley-man waved her to walk in front of his streetcar, but she did not acknowledge his helpful gesture. In her world any sign of kindness did not exist for her; it was always for someone else.

I looked back after the trolley continued on and saw her cross the street, walking as if it did not matter where she went. And it didn't. God help her...it just didn't matter.

About the Author

DAN TURNER grew up on the south side of Chicago with the prairie in his back yard. His spirituality and mysticism were fostered in those tall grasses, alive with butterflies, bees, and mystery. Ordained a priest in the Dominican order of preachers, he embraced the community lifestyle of the brothers. He continued his vocation as a trainer of probation officers at the Cook County Juvenile Court in Chicago, as a social activist for human justice, and as a leader in global and local pilgrimages. He made visits to Central America and participated in the Interfaith Pilgrimage for Peace and Life (from Auschwitz to Hiroshima); the Pilgrimage of the Middle Passage (from Amherst, MA to New Orleans); and the Pilgrimage for California Prison Reform. He edited *Creation Spirituality* magazine in Oakland, CA and is a co-author of *Ashes and Light*, an account of the Interfaith Pilgrimage for Peace and Life.